A Sixty-Watt Las Vegas

Mike Di Placido is a poet based in North Yorkshire. An ex-professional footballer and England Youth International, Mike 'peddled his soccer wares' across the globe, from York City to Australia and New Zealand, before turning to a life of literature – eventually taking an MA in Poetry while working as a househusband.

His debut pamphlet of poetry, *Theatre of Dreams*, was published by Smith/Doorstop in 2009, taking its title from his magical trial with Manchester United in the early seventies. He lives in Seamer, near Scarborough, with his wife and two daughters.

A Sixty-Watt Las Vegas

Mike Di Placido

Valley Press

First published in 2013 by Valley Press
Woodend, The Crescent, Scarborough, YO11 2PW
www.valleypressuk.com

ISBN: 978-1-908853-26-4
Cat. no.: VP0045

Copyright © Mike Di Placido 2013

The right of Mike Di Placido to be identified as the
author of this work has been asserted in accordance with
the Copyright, Designs and Patents Act 1988

All rights reserved. No part of this publication may be
reproduced, stored in or introduced into a retrieval system,
or transmitted in any form, by any means (electronic,
mechanical, photocopying, recording or otherwise) without
prior written permission from the rights holders.

A CIP record for this book is
available from the British Library

Printed and bound in Great Britain by
Imprint Digital, Upton Pyne, Exeter

This book is sold subject to the condition that it shall not,
by way of trade or otherwise, be lent, resold, hired out,
or otherwise circulated without the publisher's prior
consent in any form of binding or cover other than that
in which it is published and without a similar condition,
including this condition, being imposed on the
subsequent purchaser.

www.valleypressuk.com/authors/mikediplacido

Contents

Diktat Song 9
Cleo 10
About this time last Friday 11
Valley Bridge 12
Undertaker 13
Czar Lepke 14
The Assassin 15
Heron 16
Uncles 17
Reading Room 18
Solar 19
A Hoover in August 21
Hare 22
Scarborough Castle 23
Spring Bank 25
A Poet Practices for the Lectern 26
Meeting T.S. 27
Meeting Ted 28
Meeting Simon 30
Not Meeting Dickens 31
To R.S. Thomas 32
Nostradamus 33
I Dreamt I Was On A Tram In San Francisco 34
Free 36
Albert 37
The Vic 38
Alfie's Magic Wand 39
Recovery 40
Where Eagles Dare 41
Invitation 42

Acknowledgements

Many thanks to the following where some of these poems first appeared: *The North, The Rialto* and *Pennine Platform*. 'Solar' was shortlisted for The Bridport Prize, 2012.

Special thanks are due to Martin Arnold for his early and unceasing support of my writing; to Mathew Pateman for suggesting *A Sixty-Watt Las Vegas* as a possible title; to Steve Ellis and Ron Taylor for their help and support over the years; to Ann Stewart at *poetry p f*; to Peter and Ann Sansom for everything; to Dave Vallance; to my wife, Donna, and my daughters, Charlotte and Tiffany – mainly for putting up with me! And, lastly, a huge thank you to Jamie McGarry at Valley Press, for 'getting' the *Sixty-Watt* idea, and thus enabling me to realise my long held ambition of producing a work in celebration of my home town of Scarborough.

All that I write and do is in loving memory of Mum, Dad, and Christine.

The quotations 'bleak north' and 'that that little is more than enough' (p. 32) are taken from R.S. Thomas's collection, *Counterpoint* (Bloodaxe Books, 1990).

*for
Peter & Ann
Sansom*

Diktat Song

Some people are bad for the soul. Avoid them.
I quote granddad: *Never wrestle with chimneysweeps.*

Notwithstanding how they were 'wired up'
Best, then Gascoigne, were Britain's finest.

There's no such thing as a *slight* untruth. All lies
tilt – however marginally – the axis of the earth.

Of the crooners, only *one* led the way:
Sinatra. Accept this as a given.

But do tell me this: what greater bargain
than *Manhattan* for 50p at the video store?

And when the moors whip the top of your head off
and you see like a kestrel: what else is there?

Great moments in history: The Big Bang, the invention of the wheel,
Diego's second against England in Mexico, '82. (And also his first.)

But always remember this: when someone's lying to you
their unsmiling eyes will be saying: *you do not exist.*

Cleo

after Christopher Smart's 'Jubilate Agno'
for Eric and Andrea

Eviscerated any small rodents
lately? Tortured any mice?
Had a few tidy dumps in the rose beds?

She just purrs, regards me
with those Liz Taylor eyes,
then spins and glides up the garden,

without so much as a backward glance.

About this time last Friday

it was bright, busy and warm.
Car windscreens flashed to each other.
A woman in a wheelchair made for the post office.

A policeman was talking to a fat man in a tank top
and two gorgeous black girls in shorts
wiggled down the precinct from Tesco.

Music blared out near McDonald's
as two kids were led from the Brunswick
by helium dinosaurs lashed to their wrists.

Shoppers were in hive mode. High street benches
filled with people munching sarnies.
Others stood lobbing loose change

into the mime artist's real hat
as he edged along an imaginary plate glass window
opposite the mannequins in Ann Summers.

The sun was playing *now you see me*
and every so often with the passing of a cloud
a tree's fret-worked print would brand the pavement

like an affirmation of *this* moment *now*
or some new installation at Tate Modern.

Valley Bridge

'The final stages of safety work designed to prevent suicides on Scarborough's notorious Valley Bridge are underway.'
– Scarborough Evening News, 13th March 1991

At least it's safe to walk across now:
those barriers as much a comfort as defence
against any mad impulse to jump
or swallow-dive into the blue.

Now you're snug – smug, in fact –
caged into life, as you promenade
beneath the hanging baskets
or stop in the middle to look at the view.

And if you ever walk or drive underneath –
especially on a sunny day –
it's hard to believe you're in an open crypt,
until you see all those ghosts, marking time,

milling around the lily-pond.

Undertaker

for Martin Threapleton

You almost wanted to sign up early –
put yourself in his hands.

With his gnarled benevolence
and graveyard humour

you knew the job would be sorted
as soon as you made that first call.

Okay, a tidy ceremony may not be
the answer to everyone's prayers,

but when the pressure was on,
he seemed like some rugged saint,

who was not only more capable,
but knew exactly what to do –

just when you needed it most.

Czar Lepke

after Robert Lowell's 'Memories of West Street and Lepke'
(Life Studies, 1959)

It was the hands you noticed, first:
hanging passively and cuffed by denim,
radiating their history. Lepke:

regarded as a God, his unchallenged gaze
sweeping inmates from his path –
from his halo of space.

Judgement day arrived with the anaesthetic,
from then on life was all clear-cut –
the buds of memory secateured.

Now, marking time with work
in the laundry, he waits for his *special* day.
And those times in his cell,

when the angles are correct
and the sunbeam finds him,
he's so radiant in the corner, all lit up and happy,

like a sort of premonition.

The Assassin

You've got to hand it to him,
he's a real artist, so versatile,
a master of extemporization.

Meets us on a morning
with coffee and papers,
then lulls us to sleep of an evening.

When he makes a decision, someone's
out of the ball game for good –
and he's not bothered how it's done:

in sleep, that trip down the stairs,
those wet fingers on a dodgy plug.
Can be ruthless, too, on a grander scale –

pulling off the big stunt just to show who's boss:
that airliner, some ingenious disease,
genocide in Africa.

But has he got a soft spot? Conscience,
perhaps, when he bides his time
on a mortgaged soul, extending the expiry.

We often think he's got nothing to say,
but in a way he *does* answer us
when we interrogate the arid silence –

punctuated by bird song, perhaps,
or the rumble of a washer – silence *is* his answer,
knowing we can understand no more.

Heron

You wouldn't be surprised if you heard
the clanking of metal when he took off.

Perhaps you've wandered into Jurassic Park?
Ridiculous, this gangling oddball.

But not that skewer of a beak
you imagine a fish seeing

through the shattering glass,
the whirl of water.

Uncles

Always so helpful weren't they? And wise.
Knew what to do with a breakdown
– best garage for repairs,
what the car was like for spares.

And never shy.
They'd laugh out loud
or go around shaking hands.
And at Christmas you'd smell drink
when they talked to you
or patted you on the back.

They'd ruffle your hair or wink,
or make silly noises, and their wives
would sit with hats on and knees together
while the port and sherry went round.

Sometimes uncles looked serious or sad
then they'd suddenly cheer up again
and you'd wonder what it was they'd seen.

Whatever happened to uncles? Where did they go?
Did they die out like the dinosaurs
or are they all in cryogenic suspension?

I think of this as I look for my slippers,
search for Radio 4;
recognise my sister's kids
banging at the door.

Reading Room

for all at Scarborough Library

You always get one or two in here: like precious specimens
blooming in the warmth, they sit, frowning over books
or stand nonplussed by the photocopier.

That one's been coming in for years: his face
out of sync, now, with his ponytail,
but the same nervous tic as he scans *his* TLS.

But there's my favourite: like some theatre luvvie,
permanently between productions, he pores over the
 broadsheets
before rummaging in the bowels of Reference.

And the librarian sits, serene in her benign authority.
Only the quarrelling of gulls gets past her,
through the high, half-open window.

Then on rising to leave (as though pushing off
from deep water), I'm noticed by keen eyes
near the microfiche, as I drift towards the sunlit exit

to surface on the raucous streets.

Solar

With the first rays, we ransack the shed for those stripey
   chairs from Asda.
Supine in *RayBans* and ridiculous raiment, we incant his
   name.

We coat alabaster limbs with lotion and sun block from
   brightly coloured bottles.
We dream of Cap Ferrat and Cannes; of moonlit walks after
   balconied dinners;

of posing shamelessly in white linen and canvas loafers.
   I'm George Clooney
at the Carlton Hotel with four starlets. (My wife dreams of
   George, too.)

Of course, we don't want skin cancer! But neither do we
   wish to remain blue-veined
and translucent. We check the number on the bottle (as
   we've been told), though secretly

worried we'll scupper our tan. In gardens and patios, we
   affect 'A' list personas –
sipping daft drinks with little umbrellas – then go loopy
   when sun cream's splodged

over *The Guardian*. Our children disappear under headgear
   with built-in visors
but re-emerge as if by magic when the sarnies come out.
   Sooner or later, of course,

his majesty retires, as do we. Then back inside, blinking
    and slightly sore, we re-adjust
to the telly, and re-stock with Cif, from the corner shop, to
    wash tidemarks from the bath.

A Hoover in August

The fridge hums to keep him company,
the table fends off light beams, the microwave
entertains him with the family's comings and goings;
and often a leg, connected to a man, woman
or little girl's foot kicks him – but he doesn't mind.

Morning's his time: dragging his owner
round the room, he bosses the carpets
or extends down the backs of chairs, sofas;
and though he's never used to vac the car
he often wonders what the outside world is like.

This month is sand. He's already had a belly full –
mixed with the usual fluff and grit –
and while they're at the beach, he waits:
can't see the sun, only its translation into light
and shadows on the walls, the side of the cooker,

the lightening and deepening of the tiled floor.

Hare

Alone
in a fallow field
as though he can't be seen.
(And you amazed, again,
at just how big they are.)

Not the brightest of course:
like jay-walking pheasants
or partridges, losing it,
just when the gun's being cocked.

But you *really* like him. Just know
he'd be a riot if he could talk –
how well you'd get on.
And those semaphore ears!

Now he's off again:
going like the clappers
over the furrows, doing that
buckled
bicycle wheel number

as though
just for the hell of it. As though,
even through
those clenched gnashers,

he just can't keep it all in.

Scarborough Castle

Still ruling the roost:

with the old town

The keep's looking

and below the walls

from dark-age ditch

But you're thinking

and its breaching:

spotting the beach,

on the obedient surf:

and whale-road

slicing through resistance

bloodstream.

night in 400AD:

among the stars,

longing for family

guarding both bays

in her skirts.

suitably weathered

the moat has morphed

to children's playground.

of a sentry-scanned horizon

of a dragon's head

then riding towards it

the world-serpent

negotiated – and them:

to enter an island's

Or some bone-cold

signal station lookouts

cursing and stamping,

and olive groves.

Castle hill's seen it all:
                    the bark of Norman masters;
the shamble of serfs,
                    where a town develops
like a print in a darkroom.
                    It's three thousand years BC:
they'll dig you up a few
                    millenia from now –
but today, you're looking
                    over bronze-age bays and inland
as far as the eye can see –
                    which is why you're up here, of course:
security comes with ocean
                    and cliffs wrapped around you.

Fast forward to 2012.
                    I'm on the Esplanade
under one of Hardy's
                    full-starred heavens that winter sees;
looking down at the bay
                    and the spangled seafront –
a sixty-watt Las Vegas –
                    and then up at you,
suspended in black space,
                    like the limb of some great starship.

Spring Bank

South Bay, Scarborough, 2010

Knee-deep in the North Sea's
crash and drag
I'm one of Antony Gormley's sculptures.

(Looks as though I'm the furthest one out.)

Like some clueless ambassador,
meeting that which is coming towards us
with whatever it is we have to offer.

A Poet Practices for the Lectern

I declaim my latest verse
to the washer, the table, and the parrot

who repeats the last two syllables
of the last line of each stanza

(though not with the authority
I would wish for at a reading).

The empty house is witness
to expansive gestures and posturing,

in front of mirrors, tables, and armchairs
until – and I'm almost *certain* of this –

it begins to applaud.

Meeting T.S.

for Steve Ellis

He'd enter unobtrusively, hang up his coat,
then wander over in his *four-piece suit*.
At one of those dimly-lit tables we'd talk,

he'd clean his specs, but it was his questions
that intrigued: never politics or anything specific,
but always aware of some great thing moving against us.

Once, when I said I loved parts of *The Wasteland*
but that he was spot-on in 'Journey of The Magi',
I could have crawled to the toilets and opened a vein.

He'd smile, as if to help me in some way,
but when I confessed to little Italian and less Dante
his silence said it all.

And when he was stood at the hat-stand
getting ready to go, I felt as though I'd been visited
by something from beyond my horizon:

me at the mouth of a river,
fishing from a boat with a hand-line,
then some cliff of steel cancelling the sun and him:

Tony Curtis's Cary Grant in *Some Like It Hot*,
leaning over the handrail
and booming through a megaphone

asking the way to civilisation.

Meeting Ted

Striding up the track opposite Lumb Bank:
you. Larkin's *Easter Island statue*
in waterproofs, enlarging towards me.

Shamelessly, I effect an introduction.
Talk about the snake I'd just seen
which you immediately name. I listen,

keep schtum about my poetry,
say how much I admire yours
then mention Scarborough. Had you been?

A Pennine version of *Midnight Cowboy*:
my Ratso Rizzo to your gortexed Joe Buck
shuffling to keep up. Then you're gone;

so I follow your parting wave
and diminishing outline,
'till they're finally swallowed by the wood,

then imagine you casual in jacket and slacks,
looking in antique shops; prowling around
the museum or strolling on the East Pier.

Some big loner on a day at the seaside…
Fat chance! (But the idea appeals.)
Perhaps you'd slip into the pictures:

I see you wedged into a bucket seat,
that huge frame jack-knifed in the circle,
about to lose yourself – your conscious self –

in some movie. I see the lights go down,
you settling into delicious anonymity –
your mind engaged in cosmic dramas.

Then that great ham of a hand; pincering
the little plastic fork, as it slices, curd-like,
the top layer of your raspberry fruit parfait.

Meeting Simon

The Oak Rooms, Byram Arcade, Huddersfield: 13th June 2008

We were getting on famously 'till I started to choke –
too many fluffy nibbles and not enough tea.
It's Italian, I croaked, as he queried my surname,
but I don't usually sound like the Godfather!

Thank God he laughed (even if he didn't mean it)
adding (and perhaps it was the pin-stripe)
that I did have a look of the Al Pacino
about me. This I took as a compliment

and not some marker of perceived threat.
Then he was gone: *Time to melt into
the Huddersfield air,* he said, poetically,
leaving me wondering if he ever took a night off

and if I'd upset him somehow? Pictured him
padding up the darkening lane to Station Street,
nervously checking over his shoulder
as he made his way back to his golden life.

Not Meeting Dickens

'In 1858, Charles Dickens gave two readings at the Assembly Rooms in Huntriss Row, currently the site of Pizza Hut.'
– The History of Scarborough, Jack Binns

And if you've the gift
(as you eat with the family
or stare out the window with a drink),

you could well look up and see
the man himself, hard at it at the lectern,
all flying hair and gimlet-eyed:

the graveyard scene
with Magwich, perhaps?
Or Bill Sykes throttling poor Nancy.

'Till looking up
at people scoffing pizzas,
or kids up and down to the loos,

he seems to lose it,
grabbing his papers
before storming off stage

and through the doors
to Huntriss Row,
losing himself on the scrambling streets.

To R.S. Thomas

'If poetry can't cope with what God means in the late twentieth century, then it doesn't deserve to be regarded as a major art form.'
– R.S. Thomas (The Independent, Saturday 27th February 1993)

I was wondering if, towards the end,
faith's compass had failed you?
Whether its *bleak north* proved illusory
(the needle going haywire
in some terrible
re-configuration). I hope not.

I hope it stayed true to its promise
(though trembling as those needles do);
that what you met there vindicated utterly
the journey towards that
which you'd divined on your peninsula
(as near to heaven as could be without touching)

or in your verse: those chiseled, austere,
persistent attempts to explain the unexplainable;
views now deemed, at best, 'old hat',
precisely because of that.

Perhaps, though, you'd found it all along –
the journey (not the destination) being the point.
In perfecting your art, you perfected yourself,
knowing

that that little is more than enough.

Nostradamus

He couldn't have enjoyed his gift. Imagine:
knowing the one who'll give you herpes
(or worse); that over there's the burger bar
that's going to leave you heaving for a week!
And you couldn't put a bet on or go fishing:
winning all the time would bore you rigid
and what to do between the expected
bites and nibbles on your line?
You'd be a nervous wreck, anticipating
toothaches, dead legs, bashing funny bones...
paranoid too: called a prat behind your back
then smiled at – and that's from your mates!

Then the big stuff: plagues, earthquakes, eclipses,
the Antichrist arriving by taxi. He didn't need it!
Got pissed off, being the high priest of prescience,
nights waking up in a cold sweat because
some prince or pope's about to croak it.
So he decided enough was enough: retired
to a place in the country where he cultivated
amnesia. Settled for the obvious:
full moons, sunrises, sunsets,
winters unlocking into summers;
took himself off the hook, grew cabbages,
changed his name.

I Dreamt I Was On A Tram In San Francisco

It was summer. Warm.
I'd a pair of Bermuda shorts on
and one of those large, brimmed hats –
I *never* wear hats – and Jesus sandals.

The street was *that* street
from the car chase in *Bullit* –
so it was a hill, really –
and although I scoured the bay
for a view of Alcatraz,
I couldn't really see it
because of a pocket of mist.

People were sauntering past
in Hawaiian shirts
and talking *very* loudly.

Then *he* passed by,
the man himself – Thom Gunn!
(T-shirt and jeans, scuffed shoes, battered briefcase.)

Off to a boyfriend's?
To teach?
A reading, perhaps?

He was still alive then
I think,
but I couldn't really say,

because that's the trouble
with those dreams,
that put you on trams, in summer,

in San Francisco.

.

Free

A 'Free Transfer' occurs, in professional football, when a club decides not to exercise its option to renew a player's contract.

Just four short lines
delivered in a brown buff envelope.
(I remember that envelope.)

Their loss not mine! To dad's silence
by the kitchen sink, the day before
the cup final: Leeds v Sunderland, 1973.

Then later, blind with drink:
I'm gonna try Barcelona next!
as friends walked away in the pub.

Then thirteen years of the same –
about the length of a career, actually –
'till, blinking in the light, at thirty-one,

to hack around in the Sunday leagues.
Lost years? Wasted years?
Or maybe just the time it took

for a clueless nineteen-year-old kid
to find his way back.

Albert

The Norbreck Hotel, Scarborough, 1968

Poached from a paper round
to be a porter's assistant –
your assistant, weekends and holidays –
I worked there because you worked there.

Everybody loved you: small, skinny,
National Health specs; probably mid-fifties,
but to me, at fourteen, you were Methuselah.
And so funny! You'd slap a trailing leg to bring it in line,
or chase a pea around your plate, moaning
how hard life was – that even your vegetables
were giving you the runaround.

A Bradford man, you were football mad,
which explains why, four years later,
you turned up at Valley Parade to watch me play.
We met after the game: *You did all right lad…*
but then you would say that.
Then we lost touch. As you do.

Until today that is, when, walking down
memory lane past the hotel, I see you staring
owl-like through a window,
waiting for the coaches to arrive.

The Vic

Early for the reunion,
I reclaim my old corner stool, look

in the mirror behind the optics,
and watch myself enter, singing Sinatra.

The barmaids smile, refuse proposals –
including marriage – and pull the pints.

He's amazed at my Coke, regards it as
witchcraft, some potion ringed by garlic

and wants it replaced. I politely refuse,
then he's off, talking to anyone who'll listen

'till they, too, turn away, leaving him with
his only option: the door and the night.

Alfie's Magic Wand

for my godson, Alfie Dancy

He started to cry when he first saw me,
which I took as a positive sign –
nice to be taken seriously.

Then he settled down and wouldn't stop
smiling. Due no doubt to the strip of foam
he was waving around and wouldn't let go of.

I was taken with the white piano and the bookshelves
as we sat around nattering and drinking tea
while Alfie conducted proceedings.

He'll be fine. After all, what can the world
do to you when you're armed with a magic wand
and that title: Alfie, Alfred, Alfredo –

my father's name.

Recovery

So you've pieced back
together your heart,
re-inserted those eyes
(that now see like a falcon)
and replaced the top of your skull.

Now take great gulps
of this incredible, fresh, new air;
blink into that
cauterising light
and laugh,
            laugh,
laugh out loud;

then start to *win*.

Where Eagles Dare

I've nobbled Richard Burton
because I want his voice. I want
to say – have *always* wanted to say:

Broadsword calling Danny Boy.
Broadsword calling Danny Boy.

I want to curl my lip like his.
I want to squint slightly, flare
my nostrils then growl:

Broadsword calling Danny Boy.
Broadsword calling Danny Boy.

And Clint. Clint Eastwood.
I want to order fresh-faced Clint
around and say repeatedly:

Broadsword calling Danny Boy.
Broadsword calling Danny Boy.

In fact, after a while,
because of my dearth of lines
I'm rumbled. But I don't mind.

I've become Richard Burton,
doing a Richard Burton,
in a Richard Burton movie.

Invitation

One day
it *will* happen –
that Italian feast in the garden:

long tables
under pergolas
clustered with grapes;

pasta, vino, dancing
and music – oh yes – definitely music;
Gigli, Pavarotti *and* Sinatra, capisce?

But most importantly, on the guest list, you.

And when the stragglers
are laughing down the lane
to their taxis and cars,

we'll sit
by the little gnarled apple tree,
as thudding moths shake the lanterns,

and I'll thank you, then,
with the backing of the open heavens
until the dying of the last star